OREGON TRUFFLE FEASTS

Charles Le Fevre

OREGON TRUFFLE
◆F E A S T S◆

Dawn Meiklejohn

With help from her dog, Lidia

About the Author

Dawn Hutchins Meiklejohn studied under the loving tutelage of Loretta Viola Patnode, Principal at My Granny's Knee Cooking School.

Loretta insisted good cooks started in the earth, collecting wild berries, greens and nuts. What wasn't in the fields and woods was grown in the garden, first tilling the soil, planting the seeds, watering the sprouts, fertilizing with compost, tea leaves and coffee grounds; weeding and harvesting. How sweet were the fruits of those labors!

Fun at the end of a long day was tagging along with the neighbor to bring the cows in for nightly milking and carrying home two quarts of fresh raw milk for breakfast.

The larder was stocked with canned goods from the summer's bounty. Fresh homemade bread, cake doughnuts, and sugar cookies, some with an almond and others with a raisin in the center, filled the pantry. The pie safe held the tasty fruit delights.

How could Dawn not spend the rest of her life feasting and sharing those feasts with others!

OREGON TRUFFLE FEASTS.
Copyright 2016 by Dawn Meiklejohn.
All rights reserved. Printed in the United States of America.

Design:
Jason Black and Bob Hutchins

Photography:
Food: Paola Thomas
Lidia: Paola Thomas
Truffles: Oregon Truffle Festival
Georgia Freedman
John Valls
Charles Lefevre

ISBN: 0692787127
978-0692787120

To my granddaughters, Laura Johanna Mack and Heidi Regina Mack
For inspiration
And gratitude
My enthusiastic sous chefs, foragers, and dog trainers

Georgia Freedman

Contents

Charles Le Fevre

Acknowledgements

To The Honorable Randall R. Rader, former Chief Judge of the United States Court of Appeals for the Federal Circuit, who was the first to needle me to write this book.

To Sunny Diaz and her Lagotto Romagnolo, Stella, who have shared fun times with us foraging, and tasting, and offered the necessary critical eye.

To Paolo Thomas the fabulous photographer whose enthusiasm for foraging with dogs and creative eye makes the food look mouth wateringly delicious.

To Bob Hutchins for always being the helpful brother that saves me on my art projects.

To Charles Lefevre, Ph.D. and Leslie Scott of The Oregon Truffle Festival who have been there with support and encouragement.

To John Kelly, Langdon Cook, Brooke Fochuk, Launie Fairbairn, Cambria Cox, Marjorie Fielding and Cindy Oliveto who have shared their knowledge.

To Bridget Flynn of Lagotto Kennels for breeding and choosing Lidia for me.

To all my tasters who helped me decide whether to keep, tweak, or toss the recipes.

To my husband, my biggest supporter, Paul Meiklejohn.

John Valls

Introduction

Oregon Truffle Feasts features recipes specifically for the truffles native to Northern California, Oregon, Washington and Southern British Columbia. Generically, we call them Oregon Truffles; the scientific names are Tuber Oregonense and Tuber Gibbosum for our spring and winter white truffles and Leucangium Carthusianum for our black truffle.

Truffles are fruits of fungal mycelium that grow underground in a symbiotic relationship with the roots of certain species of trees. The Oregon truffles form their relationship with Douglas Fir trees.

Unlike mushrooms that drop spores from the caps for reproduction, truffles depend on truffle eaters to spread the spores. To let all members of the animal kingdom know they are ripe, truffles give off volatile organic compounds (VOCs). Fortunately, dogs have approximately 300 million scent glands compared to man's measly 5 million. Dogs find only ripe truffles. It is that aroma, the VOCs, that we want to capture in our food. Truffles themselves have little flavor, but the aromas they share with other foods make culinary masterpieces.

I've compiled these recipes to highlight our native truffles. Most truffle recipes found in cookbooks and on the internet are for European truffles. A recipe collection was needed to highlight the aromatic flavor subtleties of the Oregon truffles. In 1977, James Beard proclaimed that the Oregon truffles were equal to their expensive European cousins. He didn't say the same, they are not, there are subtle differences. The Oregon Black truffle is fruity, some say apple/pear, some say mango, and others pineapple. The Oregon white truffles percolate garlic, cheese, and the earth.

Charles Lefevre, Ph.D. mycologist, founder of The Oregon Truffle Festival, and owner of New World Truffieres, has been fascinated with fungi since he was a child foraging with his family. He has done numerous blind taste tests and Oregon truffles always come out on top, even when he served Italian White truffles costing twenty times as much as the Oregon white truffles. In all fairness to the Italians, the Oregon truffles were probably much fresher since they didn't have to travel for days from the forager, to the wholesaler, to the airlines, through customs, before arriving at the merchant's and then put in Dr. Lefevre's refrigerator.

Nothing can compare to the aroma of a fresh ripe truffle. At a highly rated Seattle restaurant I asked the chef where he sourced his truffles. He proudly told me he imported them from France and enhanced the flavor with truffle oil. Was he in for a surprise when I invited him to my car where I had a basket of truffles found by my dog, Lidia, that morning! There was no truffle oil enhancement needed for those truffles. Capturing that aroma is what Oregon Truffle Feasts is all about.

How I Taught Lidia to Harvest Truffles

Lidia was chosen from her litter to be a Therapy Dog. At twelve weeks old she received her puppy certification from Project Canine. She had over one hundred therapy visits to hospitals, schools, and veterans' homes by her first birthday. Lidia earned both her AKC Th.D (Therapy Dog) and CGC (Canine Good Citizen) titles. She is now registered with The Alliance for Therapy Dogs. While on our visits many people inquired about her breed. When I explained that she was a Lagotto Romagnolo, an ancient Italian breed, bred in Italy to truffle hunt, the next question was always, "Does she find truffles?" The challenge was on! Lidia had been a star in her Smarty Dog Tricks class so I knew it would be easy to train Lidia. I watched several You Tube videos on truffle dog training, and started from there.

My philosophy of dog training is rewarding desired behavior. Clicker sounds reach the amygdala, the automatic survival reaction part of the dog's brain, first. The voice sounds go to the cortex or thinking part of the brain second. Dogs don't generalize well. Think of a dog that runs through their repertoire of tricks when they see you with the treats. In truffle training I wanted Lidia to accomplish only one specific task and I wanted her to do it with enthusiasm so I used a clicker and treats.

I stood on my back deck with a container holding a cotton ball soaked with local truffle oil. I put the container near Lidia's nose, clicked and treated. I repeated this about five times. (This process is called imprinting.) Next I put the container on the floor next to me. When Lidia went to smell it, I clicked and treated. I picked up the container, waited a few seconds and put it back down on the floor near me. At the first sniff, click and treat. This was repeated several times and each time I moved it further from me. In about ten minutes after many successful truffle sniffs, I threw a party of many treats, hugs, and words of praise. Lidia deserved a break. Later the same afternoon we resumed our fun training time. I put the container further away, then on a chair, then behind the flowerpot. This game was too easy so we went to the yard. Initially, I just lay the container on the lawn. We practiced that several times, had another party and love fest ending a training session on a happy successful note.

A few minutes each day is all it took. After successfully finding the one truffle scent container repeatedly on the lawn, I added more truffle scented containers around the yard. Later, I started putting them under leaves and bushes. Within a week I was burying our artificial truffles on our property while Lidia was confined to the house. I usually let them

Truffle Hunting with Lidia

Our foraging is done mostly alone, off trails, tromping in the Douglas Fir forests. Safety is my utmost concern so I always carry my scout prepared backpack:

First Aid Kit for me
First Aid Kit for Lidia
Bear bells
Nylon ground cloth
Space blanket
Cell phone
Compass
Whistle
Water proof matches
Lighter
Mirror
Extra socks
Hat
Gloves
Plastic bags
Two days of food for Lidia and me
Two quarts of water for Lidia and me
Iodine tablets
Rain Jacket for me
(if I'm not already wearing it)
Coat for Lidia
(if she is not already wearing it)
Flashlight, extra batteries
Jack Knife
Duct tape
Super absorbent towel

And to Truffle Hunt:

High Value treats for Lidia

Spoon/trowel to remove the truffle from the ground

Container and paper towels to hold the found treasures.

permeate the soil for about fifteen minutes, but Lidia taught me that it wasn't necessary. One day I took six scented containers and buried them around our property. When I returned to the back door I heard the phone ring and in my haste to answer didn't close the door tightly. Lidia opened the door, went outside and found all six containers and brought them individually to the back door, all in less than five minutes.

Lidia's dam is a good tracking dog so to ensure that Lidia was finding truffles and not tracking me to the truffles, I enlisted the aid of my granddaughters. What fun we had! The girls loved hiding truffles and having Lidia find them. We progressed from our property to local parks. I found it was important to keep trying new areas to build focus for Lidia. I didn't want her to be distracted by other noises, scenes, or scents.

The next step was to go to truffle producing areas. Initially, I would give Lidia a sniff of a target scent that I carried and gave her a treat to let her know that if she found the scent, she would be lavishly rewarded. Now, I just have to get out her harness and long line and she knows what awaits.

Lidia knows that her harness and long line mean it is time for truffle foraging. She also knows that her bandana means it is time for a therapy visit. Lidia knows to act accordingly, depending on her uniform. On a truffle hunt she can run ahead, but on a therapy visit she must stay at my side.

The best advice I found for successful foraging is to build a relationship with Lidia. I want a dog that truly enjoys the hunt. Lidia and I must be in tune with each other. I want to bring the truffles home in one piece and Lidia needs to know that. It took patience to learn to communicate with Lidia so I know when she is on to the scent, I can anticipate the find, and I know the clear alert Lidia gives me to follow her nose and gently lift the truffle from the ground. Some days I need to accept disappointment and understand that Lidia is disappointed, too. She gets rewarded for her work effort.

While most any dog with a strong working drive can be trained to find truffles, I think the Lagotto Romagnolo is particularly keen for the job. It is an intelligent breed, easy to train, needs physical exercise and a job to use its brain. Foraging and nose work are second nature. Most Lagotti are devoted and strive to please their owners. Their compact size and water resistant curly coat are beneficial for trekking through the woods and underbrush. Lagotto Romagnolo have been bred for truffle hunting in Italy since the 19th century.

Care of Truffles

Truffles are best fresh. Three days is optimal, but they can be used for up to a week if you pamper your truffles.

When you get home from your forage:

Clean the truffles with a mushroom brush, soft paint brush, or soft toothbrush while gently washing them under softly running cold water.

Dry them thoroughly with paper towels.

Cut off any soft or damaged spots.

Wrap truffles individually in clean dry paper towel.

Place them in a glass container with lid.

Do not mix black and white truffles in same container.

Don't waste the aromas, use them. Have those glass containers contain something you want to infuse. Let the truffles work for you immediately.

Refrigerate.

Every day take the containers out of the refrigerator. Remove the truffle from the paper towel and wrap in a new paper towel.
If any soft spots have appeared on the truffle, cut it away.

I know that many Italians say to store truffles in rice. I don't do this because rice dries out the truffle. I much prefer to have my truffle infusing for me, multiplying its value by infusing something that I can freeze for months.

Infusions

Capturing the ethereal aroma of truffles and saving it is accomplished by infusion. It is really quite simple: all you need is fat! Fats love to absorb and keep the truffle aromas; oils, butter, cream, cheese, eggs, avocados, charcuterie, nuts, even fatty fish like salmon absorb the aroma.

Truffles don't stay fresh long. You can freeze them, but the texture changes. If you want to have something "truffle" a week, a month, six months or even a year from now, infuse the basic ingredients, freeze those ingredients and have a truffle feast after the season ends.

Another reason to infuse is the cost of truffles. If you and your dog are not finding truffles, you probably will pay about $50 for an ounce of dog found truffles. You could shave it over your pasta tonight or use that same ounce to infuse a pound of butter, a dozen eggs, a pint of cream, 2 cups of nuts, 1/2 pound charcuterie and throw an awesome dinner party in three days.

Truffles never actually touch the food I infuse. First, if I keep the truffle separate during the infusion process, I can use it for something else. Second, I am very cautious with food safety, botulism in particular. Botulism is a bacterium that produces neurotoxin spores. Botulism is present in the soil and it produces the toxins in anaerobic conditions (low oxygen). Dropping a truffle in a bottle of oil is not a risk I'm willing to take. Botulism poisoning has almost been eliminated in the United States, however food borne botulism has been most often related to lax home canning practices.

TRUFFLE INFUSED MILK OR CREAM

Glass jars or jugs with caps

Tea balls

Unwaxed, Unflavored Dental Floss or cooking string

Whole milk

Cream

Half and Half

1 truffle (black or white)

The tea ball will be suspended in the jar/jug over the milk or cream and the cap must be screwed on. If the chain or suspension device on your tea ball prevents the cap from screwing on, tie dental floss or string on the tea ball or chain.

Wrap fresh truffle in paper towel. Place wrapped truffle in tea ball. Pour milk or cream in jar or jug, leaving room for suspended tea ball. Suspend the truffle tea ball over the milk. Allow chain/string/dental floss to hang over the top of the jug/jar and hold it while screwing on the cap.

Always change the paper towel on the truffle every day. By the third day, the cream/milk will be infused and you can use the truffle for another recipe.

TRUFFLE INFUSED NUTS

Nuts in order of most fat grams per ounce of nuts:

Macadamia	21.5
Pecans	21
Pine nuts	20
Brazil nuts	19
Walnuts	18.5
Hazelnuts	17
Almonds	14

Nuts love to absorb the aroma of truffles; nuts are 80% fat! Adding truffle infused nuts to salads, vegetables and desserts is an easy way to highlight the truffle flavor.

Wrap a truffle in paper towel. Put it in a tea ball. Add the tea ball to a glass jar containing 2 cups of nuts of your choice. (Raw nuts absorb more flavor.) Cover and refrigerate.

After 24 hours, remove the tea ball, take the truffle out of the used paper towel and wrap it in a clean paper towel. Return to the tea ball, then the glass jar, cover, and refrigerate for another 24 hours. Repeat for a third day.

The refrigeration is necessary for the truffle, not the nuts, so after the three days of infusing, I use the truffle for another recipe and leave the infused nuts in the well-sealed glass jar in my pantry. Nuts can be in the pantry for up to six months.

Nuts that you will not be using in six months can be frozen for up to a year and still retain the truffle infused aroma.

TRUFFLE INFUSED HONEY

I have infused honey the same way I have infused other liquids, by suspending the truffle tea ball over the honey.

My experience is that the infused honey tastes delicious! However, I have not been able to keep the truffle aroma in the honey for more than three weeks. The honey reverts back to its original flavor.

I do not want to infuse using heat as the honey will lose some of its health benefits.

John Kelly, a beekeeper and fellow dog team truffle forager, had a wonderful suggestion, honey truffle butter. The fat in the butter will retain the truffle aroma.

You can infuse the butter and honey in the usual way, remove the infused butter from the refrigerator, let it soften at room temperature and then mix the butter and honey together. Return the mixture to the refrigerator or freeze. It maintains the truffle aroma and tastes fabulous.

TRUFFLE INFUSED OILS

Use an oil that does not have strong flavor overtones. You want the truffle aroma to stand on its own or to enhance the flavor of the oil. Avocado oil and extra light olive oil work well.

I infuse using white or black truffles depending on the flavor that I want.

Put one quart of oil in a two quart glass jar with tightly closing lid. Place truffle in a paper towel inside a tea ball, suspend (with string or unwaxed/unscented dental floss) tea ball above the oil in the jar. Tightly close lid. Refrigerate. Infuse for a week, changing the paper towel every day.

TRUFFLE INFUSED EGGS

6 fresh eggs in shell
1 truffle
paper towel
tea ball

Wrap truffle in paper towel, place inside a tea ball. Put eggs still in their shells in a glass container, add the truffle tea ball, cover and put in the refrigerator. The next day, remove the tea ball, unwrap the truffle, throw away used paper towel and wrap the truffle in a new piece of paper towel. Return wrapped truffle to the tea ball and put tea ball back in the egg filled glass container, cover, return to the refrigerator for an additional 24 hours.

In two days you have wonderfully infused eggs and you still have a fresh truffle that can be used for slices on your eggs, in your burger, on your truffle meatloaf and mashed potatoes, or any truffle recipe of your choosing.

If you have already hard boiled your eggs, no problem. You can infuse them the same way, either peeled or unpeeled.

TRUFFLE INFUSED BUTTER OR CHEESE

Tea ball
Paper towel
Glass dish with lid
1 pound of butter or cheese
1 truffle (black or white)

Wrap clean fresh truffle in paper towel and put in a tea ball. Put the cheese or butter (you do not need to remove butter from its paper wrapper) in the glass dish, add the truffle tea ball.

Cover and refrigerate for a day. Remove from refrigerator, take out truffle tea ball, open and remove day old paper towel. Replace with fresh paper towel. Put wrapped truffle back in tea ball. Return to glass dish, cover, and refrigerate. Change paper towel daily for three days.

The infused butter and cheese will freeze for 3 months.

WHITE TRUFFLE INFUSED CHARCUTERIE

Use Oregon white truffles to infuse charcuterie. I like to use local meats from a favorite butcher or the farmer's market. The fat from the charcuterie will absorb the umami flavor of the truffle. Place the meat and a paper towel covered truffle in a tightly sealed glass dish for three days. Every day replace the paper towel. Once the meat is infused, you can keep it in your freezer for up to a year.

The truffle infused charcuterie can be added to a fresh salad, made into a sandwich, or served on a cracker or toast point for an appetizer.

The fat from the charcuterie will absorb the umami flavor of the truffle.

TRUFFLE INFUSED ALCOHOL

Any alcohol with 80-90 proof can be infused with truffles. Both black and white truffles work well.

Place one quart of your alcohol in a two quart jar with a tightly closing lid. Wrap your truffle in a clean paper towel, place it in a tea ball, and suspend the tea ball over the alcohol. (I replace the chain on my tea ball with string or unwaxed/unscented dental floss so the lid will form a tight seal.) Close the lid and refrigerate. Every day for five days, remove the tea ball, check the truffle for soft spots, cut off if necessary, wrap the truffle in fresh paper towel, suspend the truffle tea ball in the jar, return to the refrigerator.

Jennifer Kadell and Lee Madoff of Bull Run Distilling made fabulous truffle vodka martinis at the 2016 Oregon Truffle Festival and from now on will be selling MEDOYEFF VODKA Infused with Oregon Truffles exclusively at The Oregon Truffle Festival.

Basics

TRUFFLE SALT

1 teaspoon finely
  chopped/grated black
  or white truffle

1 cup salt

Use salt of your choice. Use your black or white truffle scraps/peelings

I prefer to grind my coarse salt first before adding truffle so the truffle doesn't get stuck in the salt mill.

Add the truffle to the salt in a glass jar, cover, and shake to mix.

I keep it in the freezer so I don't worry about bacteria. It also retains the truffle aroma for months in the freezer whereas in the cabinet it loses its aroma in a couple weeks.

TRUFFLE MAYONNAISE

**Room Temperature
  Ingredients**

1 truffle infused egg yolk

2 teaspoons white vinegar

3/4 cup truffle infused oil

Both black and white truffle infusions work well with mayonnaise.

Place egg yolk, and vinegar in food processor/blender and mix well. Scrape down sides of the bowl, put lid back on and process/blend on low while slowly pouring in oil. Blend until ingredients have emulsified.

Leftover mayonnaise should be kept in tightly covered jar and refrigerated.

Time: 5 minutes

WHITE TRUFFLE AIOLI

2 cloves of garlic

1/2 teaspoon salt

juice of 1/2 lemon

2 white truffle infused egg yolks

1 cup white truffle infused oil

Put garlic, salt, juice and infused egg yolks in food processor/blender. Process/blend until garlic is minced. Scrape down sides, put the lid back on, and slowly process while pouring in the infused oil. Process until aioli emulsifies. Aioli should be smooth and thick.

Leftover aioli should be kept in a tightly covered jar and refrigerated.

Time: 10 minutes

WHITE TRUFFLE BEEF GRAVY

1/4 cup white truffle butter

beef pan drippings
 if you have them

1/2 onion finely chopped

1/4 cup gravy flour

2 cups beef broth

2 cups white truffle infused
 heavy cream

1/2 cup red wine

1 grated truffle

pepper

white truffle salt

Melt butter in saucepan, drippings, too, if you have them. Add the onion and sauté until soft. Stir in the flour, making a roux, then slowly add the beef broth, wine, and truffle infused heavy cream. Stir over low heat until thickened, add truffle shavings and transfer to a serving dish. Season with pepper and truffle salt as needed.

BLACK TRUFFLE CHICKEN GRAVY

1/4 cup black truffle
 infused butter

2 shallots finely chopped

2 cups chicken broth

2 cups black truffle infused
 heavy cream

1/2 cup white wine

black truffle salt

pepper

1 truffle

Melt butter in saucepan, sauté shallots until softened, add chicken broth and wine, slowly pour in heavy cream, stirring until gravy thickens, add truffle shavings. Pour into serving dish. Season with pepper and truffle salt as needed.

TRUFFLE NETTLE PESTO

Food Processor

2 cups of blanched nettles

2 cloves of garlic

1/4 cup of white truffle infused nuts of your choice – pine nuts, walnuts, hazelnuts, pecans

2/3 cup of white truffle infused oil

1/2 cup grated white truffle infused cheese of your choice – Romano, Parmigiano-Reggiano, or pecorino

Put a gallon size bag of nettles in 2 quarts of boiling water for five minutes to neutralize the sting. Drain and cool. Pull off the woody stems. I like to use a French press to squeeze the excess water out of the nettles.

Use the grating blade on the food processor to grate the cheese. Change to the blending blade, add the remaining ingredients and blend until smooth.

Serve on pasta, as a base for sauces, and dressings.

Time: 30 minutes. Makes: 3 cups

While on a Wild Edibles walk sponsored by the Field Trip Society, Seattle forager and author, Langdon Cook told us about using stinging nettles for pesto. I have added my truffle twist.

When Langdon makes pesto, he puts all that he will not use immediately in ice cube trays. After it is frozen, you can pop the cubes out of the tray, and put the frozen cubes in a plastic freezer bag and keep the cubes frozen until you need them.

Alcohol

WHITE TRUFFLE BLOODY MARY

3 ounces tomato juice

2 ounces white truffle infused vodka

1 teaspoon of Worcestershire Sauce

1/2 teaspoon of horseradish

truffle salt and pepper to taste

1 lemon wedge

1 white truffle shaving

cherry tomatoes

Put juice, vodka, Worcestershire Sauce, horseradish, salt and pepper in a cocktail shaker with 4 ice cubes. Shake a few times and pour liquid into a highball glass and garnish with a lemon wedge, cherry tomatoes and a shaving of white truffle

BLACK TRUFFLE PINEAPPLE RUM KISS

In a tall glass filled with crushed ice add:

1 ounce of black truffle infused rum

2 ounces of pineapple juice

1 teaspoon of superfine sugar

Stir, garnish with a wedge of pineapple and slice of lime

CHOCOLATE BLACK TRUFFLE MARTINI

In a cocktail shaker filled with ice add:

2 parts chocolate liqueur of your choice

1 part black truffle infused vodka

1 part black truffle infused half and half

Shake until chilled, pour into a martini glass and garnish with a black truffle and chocolate shavings

Appetizers

TRUFFLE HUMMUS

1/4 cup truffle tahini

juice of 1 large lemon

1 15 ounce can of garbanzo
  beans/chickpeas

3/4 teaspoon truffle salt

2 tablespoons truffle infused oil

1 tablespoon truffle infused
  honey

2 tablespoons water

truffle shavings to garnish

Hummus works well with both black and white truffles and truffle infusions.

In a food processor mix lemon juice and tahini, process until smooth. Add 1/2 of drained and rinsed beans, process until smooth. Add second half of the beans, salt, honey and truffle oil and process. Add water as needed to make the hummus creamy. Pour into serving dish. Drizzle additional truffle oil on top and garnish with grated truffle.

TRUFFLE TAHINI

1 cup hulled sesame seeds

3-4 tablespoons truffle
  infused oil

Toast the sesame seeds in a frying pan on the stovetop. When cooled, put sesame seeds and 3 tablespoons of oil in food processor and process until smooth. Add more oil as needed.

Total time for tahini and hummus: 30 minutes

BLACK TRUFFLE STUFFED DATES

8 ounce package of pitted dates

3 ounces of black truffle infused goat cheese

25 black truffle infused pecan halves

2 tablespoons of black truffle infused honey

Carefully open the dates using the slit created when the pit was removed. Fill the center with truffle infused goat cheese, place truffle infused pecan on top of cheese, and drizzle with truffle infused honey.

Makes approximately 25 date bites

Time: 30 minutes

BLACK TRUFFLE CANDIED SALTED HAZELNUTS

2 cups black truffle infused hazelnuts

1/2 cup brown sugar

1/4 cup black truffle infused honey

1 teaspoon black truffle salt

Preheat oven to 325°

In a saucepan combine sugar and honey, heat and stir until sugar dissolves. Remove from heat, stir in hazelnuts, continue stirring to cover nuts. Spread the sticky nuts on silicon or parchment covered cookie sheet, in a single layer. Toast in the oven for 10 minutes, turning once. Remove from the oven and sprinkle truffle salt all over both sides of nuts to your taste. Cool.
Store in an airtight container.

Time: 20 minutes

TRUFFLE POPCORN

Pop your favorite popcorn and mix with your choice:

Truffle butter

Truffle oil

Truffle salt

Truffle honey butter

Use black or white truffles for your infusions, both are delicious.

Or go all the way…On hot popcorn, drizzle warm chocolate truffle sauce, toss in truffle infused peanuts, and truffle salt. Mix all together.

WHITE TRUFFLE CHICKEN LIVER PATÉ

1 pound of chicken livers

3 tablespoons white truffle infused oil

1 red onion, diced

3 white truffle infused hard boiled eggs

1 tablespoon cornstarch

4 tablespoons apple brandy

1 white truffle

Sauté onion in oil until soft, add the liver and cook until liver reaches an internal temperature of 165°

Preheat oven to 350°

Process onions, liver, eggs, brandy, and corn starch until smooth. Grease the inside of a loaf pan with truffle infused oil. Place liver mixture in loaf pan. Set loaf pan in water filled bath in larger pan. Bake for 20 minutes. Cool.

Remove from pan, place in a glass dish with tea ball containing one white truffle wrapped in paper towel. Refrigerate. In 24 hours, remove from the refrigerator, open tea ball, unwrap truffle, throw away used paper towel and replace with fresh towel, return to tea ball and glass dish with paté. Cover and refrigerate for an additional 24 hours. Remove the tea ball. If eating the paté immediately, shave on the truffle. The paté can be refrigerated for up to a week, or frozen for several months, but do not shave on truffle until ready to eat.

Time: 45 minutes plus 48 hours to fully infuse with truffle aroma.

WHITE TRUFFLE AVOCADO DIP

1 ripe avocado

1 white truffle

1/2 cup white truffle infused
  sour cream

1 tomato

juice of 1/2 lemon

1/2 teaspoon of white truffle salt

At least 48 hours in advance, place paper towel wrapped white truffle and ripe unpeeled avocado in a covered glass dish in the refrigerator. Refresh the paper towel in 24 hours.

When Ready:
Halve the infused avocado, scoop out the pulp and mash.
Coarsely chop the tomato, add to avocado.
Finely chop the truffle, add to mixture.
Mix in truffle infused sour cream, lemon juice, and truffle salt.

Can be served with tortilla chips, corn chips, bagel chips, pita chips.

BBQ WHITE TRUFFLE OYSTERS

2 dozen fresh local oysters

1 cup white truffle
  infused butter

Preheat BBQ grill

Shuck the oysters. Toss the flat shell. Keep the oyster in the rounded side shell upright to preserve the liquid.

Top each oyster in the rounded shell with 1 teaspoon of infused butter. Place shell side down on the grill and cook until oyster edges curl, about 4 minutes. Remove from grill and serve immediately.

Serves: How much do you and your guests love oysters?
Time: How fast are you at shucking oysters?

WHITE TRUFFLE STUFFED CHERRY TOMATOES

1 pint of cherry tomatoes

1/2 pound white truffle infused finely grated mild cheddar cheese

2 tablespoons white truffle mayonnaise

white truffle shavings for garnish

Cut 1/4 from the top of each tomato and slice a tiny bit off the bottom so it stands upright on the plate. Hollow out the pulp of the tomato. Save the trimmings for cooking something else. Blend remaining ingredients in food processor until smooth. Put cheese mixture in a pastry bag and pipe into the tomatoes. Top with truffle shavings. Chill until serving.

Approximately 20 bite size hors d'oeuvres
Time: 30 minutes.

TRUFFLE BRUSCHETTA

1 baguette

6-7 roma tomatoes

1/3 cup (about 15-17) basil leaves

2 tablespoons balsamic vinegar

1 cup of black or white truffle infused mozzarella

2 cloves of garlic

3 tablespoons black or white truffle infused oil

1 black or white truffle

This recipe is tasty with black or white truffles. Use whichever truffle you wish.

Slice the baguette and toast. Chop the tomatoes, basil leaves, mozzarella, and garlic. Toss with truffle infused oil.

Top toast with tomato mixture. Crown with black or white truffle slice.

Time: 20 minutes.
Serves: 4-6

WHITE TRUFFLE BEEF HEART AND PISTACHIO PATÉ

1 beef heart

2 large onions

1 quart of beef broth

2 cups of Syrah

3 tablespoons Worcestershire
Sauce

1 cup white truffle
infused butter

5 ounces of shelled raw white
truffle infused pistachios

Have your butcher open the heart and remove vessels. In a large slow cooker, put onions cut into fourths on the bottom. Top with the opened heart, add broth, wine, and Worcestershire Sauce. Cook on high for five hours. Remove heart from slow cooker. Cool until you can handle heart. Cut off any fat. Slice into eighths.

In food processor, put in four pieces of heart, and the butter. Process until smooth, add remaining heart and about 1/2 of the onions from the pot. Process again until smooth. Add the pistachios and process just until the pistachios are coarsely chopped.

Keep in tightly sealed glass dish in refrigerator.

Serve on white truffle buttered toast points or crackers of your choice.

Time: 6 hours including time in the slow cooker and cooling prior to processing.

WHITE TRUFFLE VEGETABLE DIP

1 cup white truffle
infused sour cream

2 tablespoons horseradish

1 teaspoon Worcestershire Sauce

1/2 teaspoon celery seed

1/2 teaspoon salt

1/4 teaspoon smoky paprika

2 teaspoon chopped pimento

Mix all ingredients together. Chill. Serve with a variety of mushrooms and vegetables.

Time: 5 minutes, plus time to prep fresh vegetables.

BLACK TRUFFLE SORREL SAUCE

3 tablespoons black truffle infused butter

2 cups sorrel leaves

1/2 cup chives

1/2 cup black truffle infused heavy cream

Melt the butter in a sauté pan. Add the sorrel leaves and chives, stir over heat until leaves and onions wilt and are coated with butter. Pour in the infused cream and stir over medium heat until cream coats the back of the spoon.

I learned the basics of this treasure from Langdon Cook, Seattle author and forager. I just added my truffle diamond.

BLACK TRUFFLE LEMON DILL SAUCE

1/2 cup black truffle infused sour cream

1/2 cup black truffle infused cream

juice of 1/2 lemon

1 teaspoon fresh dill snips

Mix the black truffle infused sour cream and cream with the lemon juice and fresh dill. Warm over low heat.

Mains

BLACK TRUFFLE GRILLED SALMON

**2 pounds black truffle infused
salmon filets or salmon steaks***

black truffle salt

Preheat the grill and lightly oil.
Place salmon on grill skin side down, sprinkle with truffle salt, and cook to an internal temperature of 135°.

Plate the salmon and top with sauce of choice.

Time: 20 minutes. Serves: 4

*I prefer my salmon as fresh as possible. I buy my salmon in the morning and put it in a covered dish with the black truffle until I'm ready to cook it. In as little as 5 hours the salmon has a subtle, but delicious truffle flavor.

GRILLED HALIBUT WITH WHITE TRUFFLE HAZELNUT BUTTER

4 one-inch thick halibut steaks

**1/2 cup white truffle
infused butter**

**1/2 cup white truffle
infused hazelnuts**

Preheat the grill, lightly oil. Place steaks on grill and cook until internal temperature of 135° or the fish flakes easily.

Meanwhile put hazelnuts in a plastic bag and hit a few times with a rolling pin to coarsely chop the nuts.

In a small frying pan lightly toast the hazelnuts and add the truffle butter to melt. Remove steaks from grill, plate and top with hazelnut truffle butter.

Time: 20 minutes. Serves: 4

TRUFFLE EGGS

Both black and white truffles work very well with eggs. Use what is available.

Softboiled Egg:
Put truffle infused egg in pan of cold water to cover. Bring to a boil for 1 1/2 minutes. Serve in an egg cup with truffle butter toast points

Scrambled Eggs:
Melt one tablespoon of butter in a frying pan. In a small dish crack open two truffle infused eggs, beat with a fork. Add to the melted butter and cook to desired dryness while scrambling with a fork. Serve with truffle buttered toast.

HARDBOILED EGGS

You have a choice, infuse raw eggs or hardboiled eggs, they will both absorb the flavor through the shells.

Hard Boil Egg:
Place eggs in a pan of cold water, enough to cover the eggs. Bring water to a boil, shut off heat, cover pan, let sit for 15 minutes.

A fun part of infusing eggs is that it is only the yolk that absorbs the flavors. It is a special tickle on the taste buds when you bite into a hardboiled egg.

TRUFFLE FRITTATA

1 dozen farm fresh truffle infused eggs

3/4 cup truffle infused sour cream

1/4 cup chopped flat leaf parsley

3/4 cup truffle infused gruyere cheese

Shaved truffle slices

This is delicious made with either white or black truffles, use what you have!

Preheat oven to 350°

Beat eggs with 1/2 cup sour cream, add parsley and 1/2 cup gruyere cheese. Pour into a well seasoned 10 inch cast iron skillet.
Bake for twenty minutes, remove from oven, top with remaining gruyere, return to oven just long enough to melt the cheese.

Serve with shaved truffle and a dollop of the remaining truffle infused sour cream.

Time: 35 minutes. Serves: 6-8

TRUFFLE DEVILED EGGS

6 hardboiled truffle infused eggs

1/3 cup truffle infused mayonnaise

3 teaspoons ground turmeric

black or white truffle

These are tasty with either black or white truffle infused eggs

Slice the hardboiled eggs in half lengthwise. Scoop out the yolks and place in a medium bowl. Mash the yolks, add the truffle mayonnaise and turmeric, mix well.

Spoon the yolk mixture back into the egg whites and shave truffle over egg tops.

MEAT FONDUE WITH TRUFFLE SAUCES

1 pound of top sirloin cut into bite size pieces

Cooking oil enough to fill your fondue pot 2 1/2 inches

Heat oil in fondue pot until 350°
Pierce meat with fondue fork and place in hot oil until cooked.

Dip meat in truffle sauces. (See below.)

CHICKEN FONDUE WITH TRUFFLE SAUCES

1 pound chicken cut into bite size pieces

1 cup white wine

8 cups chicken broth

Bring wine and broth to a boil
Pierce chicken with fondue fork, place in hot broth until cooked.

Dip chicken in truffle sauces.

Sauces: **Truffle mayonnaise** (see page 21)

Truffle aioli (see page 22)

Truffle gravies, beef and chicken (see page 22)

Serves: 6
Time: 30 minutes

TRUFFLE CHEESE FONDUE

clove of garlic

1/2 pound white truffle infused grated Emmentaler cheese

1/2 pound white truffle infused grated Gruyere cheese

1 cup white wine

1/4 teaspoon nutmeg

1 tablespoon cornstarch

white truffle shavings

Double boiler

Grate the cheese. Put water in bottom section of double boiler. Open garlic and wipe around the interior of the top pan. Pour wine in pan and heat. Meanwhile, dredge the grated cheese in the cornstarch and add nutmeg. Slowly add the cheese by the handful while stirring. Add a splash of wine if the fondue is too thick.

Transfer to a fondue pot on the table. Top with truffle shavings.

Serve with bread cubes or vegetables such as broccoli, carrots, and zucchini.

Time: 30 minutes
Serves: 6

WHITE TRUFFLE BEEF STROGANOFF

1 8 ounce package of egg noodles

½ cup white truffle
  infused butter

1 small onion minced

1 ½ pounds of top round steak

1 cup of sliced mushrooms

1 tablespoon flour

1 teaspoon dry mustard

1 teaspoon truffle salt

¼ teaspoon pepper

½ cup dry red wine

½ cup white truffle
  infused sour cream

chopped parsley

shaved white truffle

Prepare noodles according to the label; drain. Add 3 tablespoons of truffle butter and keep warm.

Cut round steak in half lengthwise and then into ¼ inch slices. Combine the flour, mustard, salt and pepper in a small bowl. In a 12 inch skillet, melt remaining butter, sauté the onion until tender, about 5 minutes. Add the meat and cook until slightly browned, about 3 minutes.

Add the mushrooms and dry ingredients stirring constantly, slowly add the wine, continue stirring until mixture is thickened, about 5 minutes. Stir in the truffle infused sour cream. Heat through, but do not boil. Arrange the meat mixture atop the noodles on a warm platter and garnish with parsley and shaved white truffle.

Time: 30 minutes. Serves: 6

WHITE TRUFFLE ALFREDO

1 pound fresh pasta

1 ½ cups white truffle
  infused cream

½ cup white truffle
  infused butter

½ pound of grated white truffle
  infused Parmesan cheese

chopped chives or parsley
  for garnish

shaved white truffle

Cook pasta according to directions. Meanwhile, in a saucepan heat the cream on medium, lower the heat to simmer and add the butter, stirring while it melts. Add the cheese and continue stirring. The sauce should be very creamy. If necessary add some pasta water a tablespoon at a time to keep the sauce creamy.

Drain the pasta, add to the creamy truffle cheese sauce and toss to coat.

Garnish with chives or parsley, and shaved truffle.

Time: 20 minutes. Serves: 8

WHITE TRUFFLE MEATLOAF AND POTATOES

2 pounds ground beef

1 onion chopped

3/4 cup grated white truffle
  infused Parmesan cheese

2 white truffle infused eggs

1/2 cup bread crumbs

4 tablespoons ketchup

1 tablespoon Worcestershire
  Sauce

Salt and pepper to taste

1 white truffle

White Truffle Mashed Potatoes

1/4 cup white truffle
  infused butter

Preheat oven to 350°

Beat the egg in a large bowl. Add beef, onion, 1/4 cup cheese
(save 1/2 cup cheese for later), breadcrumbs, ketchup, Worcestershire
Sauce, salt and pepper to the large bowl and mix until combined.
Place mixture in 2 loaf pans. (Meatloaf might be thinner than you
are accustomed.)

Bake the meat loaf to an internal temperature of 145°,
approximately 40 minutes.

Meanwhile prepare White Truffle Mashed Potatoes. (see page 57)

When meat is cooked, remove from oven. Place one meatloaf on
an oven safe platter. Shave truffle over the top of meatloaf. Add a
layer of truffle mashed potatoes on top of truffles, then place second
meatloaf on top of potatoes. Shave white truffle on top of second
meatloaf. "Frost" entire meatloaf, top and sides with generous layer
of potatoes. Sprinkle truffle infused parmesan on potatoes, add
dollops of truffle infused butter, return to oven to melt butter and
cheese and slightly color potatoes, about three minutes. Remove
from the oven, shave white truffle on top.

Time: 1 hour. Serves: 8

WHITE TRUFFLE BEEFALO CHEESEBURGERS

1 pound ground beef

1 pound ground buffalo

1 white truffle

8 slices of white truffle infused
  Tillamook White Cheddar
  Cheese

1/4 cup truffle aioli

8 heirloom tomato slices

lettuce

8 Ciabatta rolls

Preheat the grill. Shave the truffle, set aside

Mix the beef and buffalo together, make eight patties. Lightly oil the
grill before placing on the patties. Grill until internal temperature of
135°, remove from grill, top with a few slices of truffle, cover with
truffle infused cheese and return to grill to melt. Internal temperature
for a medium burger should be 145°.

Slice the rolls in half horizontally, and warm them on the grill.
Lightly spread aioli on roll, add the burger, lettuce, tomato, and top.

Time: 30 minutes. Serves: 8

BLACK TRUFFLE CHICKEN SALAD

4 cups diced chicken

2 cups diced scallions

1 1/2 cups cranberries

1 cup chopped celery

1 cup chopped black truffle
 infused walnuts

1 cup black truffle mayonnaise

lettuce leaves

Put all ingredients except lettuce leaves in a large bowl and mix well with a spoon. Chicken salad can be served on a lettuce leaf on a plate, or my favorite way, stuffed in cream puffs. They make bite size hors d'oeuvres in little cream puffs and nice luncheon sandwiches in large cream puffs.

Time: 20 minutes. Serves: 4

WHITE TRUFFLE OYSTER STEW

1 pint of shucked oysters

3 tablespoons of white truffle
 infused butter

1/4 cup chopped shallots

1 clove of garlic minced

2 cups of white truffle
 infused cream

4 cups of white truffle
 infused milk

Salt and pepper to taste

4 teaspoons of white truffle
 infused butter

1 truffle

Separate the oysters from the liquid. Make sure all sand is removed. Chop the shallots.

In a 4 quart saucepan, melt the butter, sauté the shallots until soft. Add the garlic, quickly stir. Slowly add the cream, milk, and oyster liquid. Simmer for 5 minutes, do not boil. Add the oysters and continue to simmer for 3-4 more minutes until the edges of the oysters curl.

Remove from heat, serve in bowls, top each bowl with 1 teaspoon of truffle butter and gently swirl. Garnish with truffle shavings.

Time: 30 minutes. Serves: 4

PUMPKIN SOUP WITH WHITE TRUFFLE CREAM

**3 sugar pumpkins
 (a 5 pound pumpkin yields
  about 2 1/2 cups pulp)**

1 quart vegetable stock

**1 cup of white truffle
  infused cream**

1 teaspoon white truffle salt

1 teaspoon white truffle oil

white truffle shavings

Cut tops off the pumpkin, scoop out the seeds. Bake the pumpkins in a 350° oven for about 45 minutes until the pumpkin is tender when pierced with a fork.

Roast the pumpkin seeds, then shell them. Slightly toast the shelled seeds. Drizzle with truffle oil.

When cool enough to handle, scoop out the pumpkin and transfer it to a food processor. Process until smooth. In a saucepan, combine the pumpkin and vegetable broth. Bring the mixture to a boil over medium heat, then lower the heat and simmer for 30 minutes. Salt to taste and slowly add 3/4 cup of the truffle cream. Continue to simmer just long enough to warm the cream, about 5 minutes.

Ladle soup into bowls, using a teaspoon swirl some of the remaining cream on top and crown with pumpkin seeds and truffle shavings.

Time: 1 hour. Serves: 8

Sides

WHITE TRUFFLE CHEESES AND GARDEN VEGETABLE SALAD

6 lettuce leaves

1/2 pound of white truffle infused cottage cheese

1/2 pound of white truffle infused ricotta cheese

1 cup grated carrot

1/2 cup diced cucumber

1/3 cup finely chopped scallions

1/3 cup chopped red bell pepper

1 chopped radish

white truffle shavings

sprig of chopped Italian parsley

Arrange lettuce leaves on a platter. In a bowl, mix cheeses and vegetables together with a spoon and spread on top of lettuce. Garnish with truffle shavings, and parsley.

Time: 30 minutes
Serves: 6

TRUFFLE CHEESY GRITS

2 cups coarse corn meal

4 cups white or black truffle infused half and half

4 tablespoons white or black truffle infused butter

1/2 cup grated white or black truffle infused cheese

shaved black or white truffle

This recipe is scrumptious with white and black truffles. If using black truffle, I prefer to use the mild Monterey Jack cheese. White truffle can stand up to a cheddar. Be consistent with your truffle: if using black truffle use black truffle infused half and half, black truffle infused cheese, and black truffle butter and the same with white truffle.

In a saucepan warm the truffle infused half and half, add the cornmeal, cook on medium heat and stir until creamy, about 20 minutes. Add the butter and continue stirring until butter melts. Remove from heat, immediately add the cheese and truffle and stir until the cheese melts. Serve hot.

Time: 30 minutes. Serves: 6

ROASTED ROOT VEGETABLES WITH TRUFFLE PECANS

1 pound parsnips

1 pound rutabagas

1 pound carrots

1 pound turnips

1/2 cup light olive oil

1 cup truffle infused
  pecan pieces

1 tablespoon of truffle
  infused oil

truffle salt and pepper to taste

This recipe is good with white or black truffle infusions.

Preheat oven to 400°

Peel and cut vegetables into 1 inch pieces, put them in a large bowl and toss with the light olive oil. Spread the vegetables evenly on two large cookie sheets. Place in the oven and roast for about an hour, turning occasionally. When the vegetables start to show brown spots, remove from the oven. Drizzle with the truffle infused oil, sprinkle 1/2 cup pecan pieces over vegetables on each baking sheet. Return to oven for three minutes to warm pecans.

Put roasted vegetables and pecans in a large bowl, salt and pepper to taste, toss to blend well and serve.

The vegetables can be prepared a few hours ahead and reheated for 15 minutes, if you wish; however, don't add the truffle oil and pecans until the last few minutes. The truffle aroma is enhanced if it is warmed, but is lost if it is too hot.

Prep time: 20 minutes. Cook time: 1 hour. Serves: 8

WHITE TRUFFLE FIDDLEHEADS

1 pound fiddleheads*,
  stems trimmed

1 clove of garlic, diced

1 tablespoon white truffle
  infused butter

1 tablespoon white truffle
  infused oil

1/4 cup grated white truffle
  infused Parmesan cheese
  (optional)

Clean the fiddleheads well in a bucket of cold water. Drain. In a 12 inch sauté pan melt the butter, add the oil and garlic, toss in the fiddleheads and cook just until fiddleheads are tender. Sprinkle on Parmesan cheese if you wish.

Time: 20 minutes. Serves 6-8.
This is great as a side dish or over pasta.

*Fiddleheads are a great bonus treasure to find when you are in the Douglas Fir forest in the spring looking for truffles. Fiddleheads are the new growth of the deciduous lady fern. Use them when they are still tightly coiled like the end of a violin.

This recipe is one inspired by Seattle forager, author and fabulous chef, Langdon Cook.

WHITE TRUFFLE RISOTTO

1 quart of vegetable or
  chicken broth

3 tablespoons white truffle
  infused butter

3 tablespoons white truffle
  infused oil

1 small onion chopped

1 1/2 cups Arborio rice

1/2 cup chardonnay

1/3 cup grated white truffle
  infused Parmesan cheese

1 white truffle

Heat the broth separately in a small pot.

In a large pan, melt 1 tablespoon of truffle butter, add 1 tablespoon of truffle oil. Add the onions, and sauté until they are translucent. Add the rice and toss to coat.

Add the chardonnay to the broth, stir. One cup at a time, add the broth/wine mixture to the pan with rice and stir until absorbed. It should take 20-25 minutes to reach the desired creamy consistency of risotto. Remove from the heat, stir in the grated infused cheese and let risotto sit for five minutes. Divide risotto into six pasta bowls and top with shaved white truffle.

Time: 45 minutes. Serves: 6

BRUSSELS SPROUTS WITH TRUFFLE ALMONDS

2 pounds brussels sprouts

4 tablespoons olive oil

2 teaspoons white or black
  truffle infused oil

1 cup white or black truffle
  infused almonds

truffle salt and black pepper
  to taste

This recipe can be used with either white or black truffles. I prefer to use the same truffle species to infuse the oil, salt, and almonds.

Clean fresh brussels sprouts, slice in half lengthwise. Heat olive oil in cast iron skillet, add a single layer of brussels sprouts to hot oil. Sear the sprouts until charred (about 7 minutes), turn over sprouts and sear other side. Remove from heat, drizzle on truffle infused oil, toss with truffle infused almonds, sprinkle with truffle salt and pepper, to taste. Serve immediately.

Time: 25 minutes. Serves: 8

WHITE TRUFFLE BRUSSELS SPROUT RAAB

Fresh brussels sprout raab

White truffle infused oil

White truffle salt

Heat a sauté pan, toss in the raab, splash with truffle oil, and sauté for 1 1/2 minutes. Remove from heat, salt to taste, and serve immediately.

SCALLOPED CHEESY POTATOES WITH TRUFFLES

3 pounds of peeled potatoes

pinch of salt

1/2 pound mild white truffle
 infused cheddar cheese

3 cups white truffle
 infused half and half

1/4 cup white truffle
 infused butter

1 white truffle shaved

parsley for garnish

Preheat oven to 350°

Peel and slice the potatoes on a mandolin or food processor. Put the sliced potatoes in cold salted water, bring to a boil, lower the heat and cook for 5 minutes.

Grate the truffle infused cheese and mix with the truffle infused half and half.

Wipe the inside of a long 12" glass dish with truffle infused butter. Layer half of the potatoes in the bottom of the dish. Pour 1/2 of the cheese/half and half mixture on the potatoes. Add a second layer of potatoes, followed by the remaining cheese/half and half mixture. Bake for 35 minutes. Remove from oven. Top with truffle infused butter slices, return to oven just to melt. Remove from oven and top with white truffle shavings and parsley garnish.

Time: 1 hour. Serves: 6-8

LINGUINE WITH CREAMY WHITE TRUFFLE ZUCCHINI SAUCE

1 pound linguine

1/3 cup white truffle infused oil

3 minced cloves of garlic

8 ounces shredded white truffle
 infused mozzarella

1/2 cup grated white truffle
 infused Parmesan cheese

1 pound of scrubbed and
 coarsely grated zucchini

1/2 cup fresh parsley

1/2 teaspoon salt

1/4 teaspoon pepper

In a large pasta kettle, cook the linguine in boiling salted water. Drain.

Return kettle to stove, add olive oil and garlic and cook for a minute. Put the pasta back in the pot and toss with garlic and oil until coated. Add the truffle infused cheeses and zucchini; continue to toss until cheese melts and zucchini coats pasta in sauce.

Serve immediately.

Time: 30 minutes. Serves: 4

WHITE TRUFFLE MAC AND CHEESE

½ pound pasta (I like shells so the cheese sauce gets in all the grooves)

4 tablespoons white truffle infused butter

¼ cup flour

3 ½ cups white truffle infused whole milk

3 ½ cups white truffle infused cheddar cheese, grated

⅔ cup white truffle infused Parmesan cheese, finely grated

white truffle

Boil pasta according to instructions. Drain and set aside.

In saucepan, melt the butter. Whisk while slowly adding the flour. Remove from heat and slowly add the milk while whisking to avoid lumps. Return to low heat and add cheddar cheese while stirring. When all the cheese has melted, add the pasta and stir to coat.

Place mac and cheese in a buttered baking dish. Top with Parmesan. Broil about five minutes to brown the top, watch it carefully. Remove from oven, shave on white truffle.

Time : 40 minutes
Serves: 4

55

BLACK TRUFFLE STUFFED SWEET POTATOES

4 sweet potatoes
1/2 cup black truffle butter
1/4 cup black truffle cream
1/8 cup black truffle oil
black truffle shavings

Bake the sweet potatoes at 425° for about an hour, until tender when pierced with a fork.

When cool enough to handle, cut the potatoes in half lengthwise, scoop out the potato. Lightly brush the skins with truffle oil and toast in oven just long enough to crisp the edges.

Mix truffle butter and truffle cream with the potato and mash with a potato masher until smooth.

Refill the potato skins with the mash and top with shaved truffles.

Time: 1 1/2 hours. Serves: 8

WHITE TRUFFLE ROASTED POTATOES

24 fingerling potatoes

4 tablespoons light olive oil

2 teaspoons white truffle infused oil

2 teaspoons white truffle salt

Preheat oven to 500°

Drizzle 1 tablespoon of olive oil on baking sheet and place in the oven to get hot.

Scrub the potatoes, dry them, then toss with 3 tablespoons of olive oil. Remove hot baking sheet from oven and spread the potatoes in a single layer. Lower the heat to 425° place the hot potato laden baking sheet into the oven and bake for 20 minutes or until fork easily pierces the potatoes. Remove from oven, drizzle with truffle oil, toss with truffle salt. Serve immediately.

Time: Prep 10 minutes. Roast 20 minutes
Serves: 8

For variety, potatoes may be French fry cut and the same recipe can be used to make baked truffle fries. Depending on the size of your fries, roasting time may be less. Check after 10 minutes.

WHITE TRUFFLE MASHED POTATOES

3 pounds potatoes

1 teaspoon salt

8 tablespoons white truffle infused heavy cream

4 tablespoons white truffle infused butter

2 tablespoons white truffle infused milk

Peel and quarter potatoes, place in pot and cover with cold salted water. Bring to a boil, reduce heat and cook for approximately 20 more minutes until fork gently pierces potato.

Meanwhile, in a small saucepan, warm the truffle infused cream and melt the truffle infused butter.

When the potatoes are done, drain the water, pour the truffle infused cream and butter mixture into the potatoes, and mash with a potato masher. Add truffle infused milk as needed to make creamy potatoes.

Time: 40 minutes. Serves: 8

Desserts

BLACK TRUFFLE FOREST TRIFLE

8 inch square pan of brownies cut into bite size pieces

1/2 cup cherry liqueur

Black Truffle Chocolate Pudding (see page 61)

16 ounce bag of frozen pitted dark sweet cherries

1 pint black truffle infused heavy whipping cream

2 teaspoons baker's sugar

small bar of chocolate

Trifle dish

Make your favorite brownie recipe. Cool the brownies and cut into bite size pieces.

Make Truffle Chocolate Pudding or your favorite chocolate pudding, but substitute black truffle infused milk for the regular milk. Use your whip cream maker, mixer, or blender to whip the truffle infused whipping cream, add the sugar to whipped cream.

In your trifle dish, layer 1/2 of the brownie bites. Slowly pour 1/4 cup of the cherry liqueur on top of the brownies. Next layer 1/2 of the Black Truffle Chocolate Pudding, then cover with 1/2 of the cherries and top with 1/2 of the black truffle infused whipped cream. Repeat the layers; brownies, liqueur, pudding, cherries, and whipped cream.

Chill in the refrigerator for at least 2 hours.
Just before serving, shave chocolate on top.

Total time: 4 hours including making brownies and pudding and then cooling.

Save time: Make the brownies and pudding ahead and assemble 2 hours before serving.

Serves: 12

BLACK TRUFFLE RICE PUDDING

1/2 cup rice

2 cups black truffle
 infused milk

1 teaspoon vanilla

1 teaspoon baker's sugar

1/2 cup black truffle infused
 slivered almonds

1 cup black truffle infused
 heavy cream

Cook rice with milk, 1/2 cup cream and vanilla, simmering over low heat, frequently stirring until the rice absorbs the milk and cream about 30 to 40 minutes. The rice should be firm, but not crunchy and the pudding will be creamy. Remove from heat and cool. Add the sugar and almonds.

Whip 1/2 cup cream and gently fold into the rice mixture.

Time: 50 minutes.
Serves: 6

BLACK TRUFFLE CHOCOLATE HAZELNUT PANNA COTTA

1 1/8 teaspoons powdered gelatin

3 tablespoons cold water

2 ounces bittersweet chocolate

1 cup Black Truffle Chocolate
 Hazelnut Spread (see page 69)

1/2 teaspoon of salt

1 1/2 cups of black truffle
 infused heavy whipping cream

1 cup black truffle infused milk

1/4 cup chopped black truffle
 infused hazelnuts

In a medium bowl whisk gelatin and cold water. Place finely chopped chocolate in a separate medium bowl. In a large electric mixer bowl, combine Truffle Chocolate Hazelnut Spread and salt.

Over medium heat in a small saucepan, bring the cream almost to a boil, watch for the little bubbles on the edges of the pan. When hot, pour half of the cream into the gelatin mixture, whisk. Pour the other half of the cream over the chopped chocolate and whisk until smooth. Combine both cream mixtures and whisk well.

Pour half of the chocolate cream mixture over the Truffle Chocolate Hazelnut Spread, beat with electric mixer until a paste forms. Pour in the other half of the mixture, add the milk, beat until everything is well combined.

Pour into six ramekins, cover loosely with plastic wrap, chill in refrigerator for at least six hours. Sprinkle with black truffle infused hazelnuts just before serving.

Time: 30 minutes, plus 6 hours chilling time
Serves: 6

BLACK TRUFFLE CHOCOLATE PUDDING

2 teaspoons vanilla extract

1/2 teaspoon espresso powder

1/2 cup sugar

3 tablespoons cocoa powder

2 tablespoons cornstarch

1/4 teaspoon salt

3 large black truffle
  infused egg yolks

1/2 cup black truffle
  infused heavy cream

2 1/2 cups black truffle
  infused whole milk

5 tablespoons black truffle
  infused butter

4 ounces bittersweet chocolate,
  grated.

Stir together the vanilla and espresso powder in a bowl and set aside. In a large saucepan, combine sugar, cocoa, cornstarch, and salt. Add the egg yolks and cream, whisk until fully incorporated. Keep whisking while adding milk.

Place the saucepan on medium heat, whisk constantly, until the mixture is thickened and bubbling (5 to 8 minutes). Remove from heat and add butter and chocolate. When they are melted, whisk in the vanilla mixture.

Pour into six dessert bowls. Cover tops with plastic wrap and refrigerate for two hours before serving.

If using the chocolate pudding for Black Truffle Forest Trifle the pudding can be put in one bowl, but should still be chilled in the refrigerator for two hours before assembling the trifle.

Time: 20 minutes, plus 2 hours for chilling. Serves: 6

BLACK TRUFFLE PANNA COTTA

1 cup black truffle infused milk

1 tablespoon powdered
  unflavored gelatin

1/3 cup black truffle
  infused honey

pinch of salt

2 cups black truffle
  infused cream

6 martini glasses or ramekins

Toppings: fruit, chocolate,
caramel, truffle infused nuts

Pour milk into a 2 quart saucepan. Sprinkle the gelatin on top of the milk and let sit for 3 minutes. Turn on medium heat and stir while warming and dissolving the gelatin, about 3 minutes. DO NOT BOIL. Add the honey and salt and continue to cook for an additional 5 minutes, again no boiling. Make sure that there is no grit (undissolved gelatin). Remove from heat, whisk in the truffle cream.

Evenly divide the mixture into the 6 martini glasses or ramekins. Cool slightly and then refrigerate for 3 hours.

Top with fresh fruit; or chocolate or caramel sauce with chopped black truffle infused nuts of your choice.

Time: 20 minutes plus 3 hours for chilling
Serves: 6

APPLE PIE WITH WHITE TRUFFLE CHEDDAR CHEESE

Pastry:
2 cups of flour

8 tablespoons milk

8 tablespoons oil

pinch of salt

2 pieces of waxed paper large
  enough to roll out pie crust

1 egg slightly beaten

Preheat oven to 350°

Put flour, milk, oil and salt in a bowl and mix well with a fork. Dough will be wetter than you think pastry crust should be. Divide the dough into two balls. Put one piece of waxed paper on the counter, sprinkle with flour, put one dough ball on waxed paper and slightly pat down, sprinkle on some flour. Top the dough with second piece of waxed paper and use a rolling pin to roll out the pastry. Drape the pastry crust in a pie plate. Roll out second pastry crust and set aside.

Filling:
3 pounds of apples, peeled
  and sliced

juice of 1/2 lemon

1/4 cup cornstarch

3/4 cup sugar

1/4 cup butter

1/2 teaspoon cinnamon

1/4 teaspoon nutmeg

In a large bowl, squeeze lemon juice on apples, add cornstarch, sugar, cinnamon and nutmeg, toss all together. Put apple mixture in pie plate on top of crust, dot with butter.

Cut vent holes in the second pastry crust and place on top of apples. Pinch the two crusts together to form a seal. Use a pastry brush to spread the beaten egg on top of the crust.
Bake for one hour in 350° oven.

Topping:
1 cup grated white truffle
  infused cheddar cheese

If you will be eating pie immediately, top with cheese and put back in the oven for a couple of minutes to melt the cheese. If the pie will be eaten later, top the pie with cheese when you warm it.

Time: 30 minutes prep, 1 hour baking. Serves: 8

My grandfather always said,
"Apple pie without cheese is
like a hug without a squeeze."

White truffle cheese is adding a kiss!

BLACK TRUFFLE HAZELNUT PARSNIP PIE

1 pastry crust

1 pound of parsnips cleaned
and cut into chunks

1 pinch of salt

2 eggs

4 tablespoons maple syrup

1 teaspoon cinnamon

1/2 teaspoon nutmeg

1/4 teaspoon ginger

3/4 cup half and half

1/2 cup black truffle infused
hazelnuts

1 tablespoon black truffle
infused butter

1 tablespoon brown sugar

1 cup black truffle infused cream

Pastry Crust:
1 cup all purpose flour

4 tablespoons oil

4 tablespoons milk

pinch of salt

Preheat the oven to 350°

Pastry Crust:
Mix all ingredients together with a fork.
Roll out between two sheets of floured wax paper.
Place pastry crust in pie plate.

Filling:
Put parsnips in a saucepan and cover with salted water.
Bring to a boil, lower heat, and cook until the parsnips
are tender, about 20 minutes. Drain and cool.

Place parsnips in mixing bowl and mash. Beat in the eggs,
maple syrup, spices, and half and half. When smooth, pour
into the crust. Bake 45 minutes until filling is set, toothpick
comes out clean when inserted in the center of the pie.

Topping:
Put hazelnuts in a plastic bag and bang with a rolling pin to
chop. Place them in shallow pan, add sugar and black truffle
infused butter and heat slowly to dissolve sugar and coat the
hazelnuts. Spread candied mixture on top of pie. Whip black
truffle cream and top each pie slice when serving.

Time: 1 1/2 hrs. Serves: 8

BLACK TRUFFLE NUT FUDGE

2/3 cup cocoa powder

3 cups sugar

1/4 teaspoon salt

1 1/2 cups black truffle infused half and half

1/4 cup black truffle infused butter

1 teaspoon vanilla

1 cup black truffle infused chopped walnuts

8 X 8 X 2 inch pan

candy thermometer

Lightly butter pan.

In a heavy 3 quart saucepan combine sugar, cocoa, half and half. Cook and stir until the sugar dissolves. Continue to cook and occasionally stir until temperature reaches 234° on candy thermometer (soft ball stage).

Remove from the heat, add truffle infused butter, do not stir. Let candy cool to 110°, outside of pan will just feel warm, not hot.

Add the vanilla, beat fudge with a wooden spoon until fudge is no longer shiny. Stir in the walnuts. Pour into prepared pan. Chill in the refrigerator for two hours. Cut into squares.

Time: 2 1/2 hours
Serves 8 – approximately
1 3/4 pounds of fudge

WHITE TRUFFLE ESPRESSO ICE CREAM

1/4 cup espresso

2 cups white truffle infused heavy cream

1 14 ounce can of sweetened condensed milk

white truffle

Cream together espresso, truffle infused heavy cream, condensed milk. Freeze in ice cream maker according to manufacturer's instructions.

Remove from ice cream maker, shave in truffle bits, put in container in freezer for 2 hours.

Time: 15 minutes prep.
2 1/2 hours wait time

Serves 8

VANILLA BLACK TRUFFLE ICE CREAM

2 cups black truffle infused heavy cream

2 cups black truffle infused half and half

2/3 cups black truffle infused honey

1 teaspoon vanilla

In a large bowl, combine cream and half and half. Use a whisk to blend in the honey.

Refrigerate for four hours, or a couple days.

When ready, whisk mixture again and pour into ice cream machine and follow your manufacturer's instructions.

Eat immediately, or put it in covered container and freeze.

Time: Minutes to blend, hours to wait.

Serves: 6

BLACK TRUFFLE CHOCOLATE ICE CREAM

1 cup black truffle infused milk

2 cups black truffle infused heavy cream

1/2 cup black truffle infused honey

3/4 cup cocoa powder

1 teaspoon vanilla

Combine all ingredients mixing well. Follow manufacturer's instructions for ice cream maker. When done remove from ice cream maker, put in airtight container in the freezer for at least 2 hours.

Time: 15 minutes prep. 2 hours waiting

Serves: 8

BLACK TRUFFLE CHOCOLATE SAUCE

4 ounces of chopped dark chocolate (always use best quality you can)

1/4 cup black truffle infused heavy cream

1 tablespoon black truffle infused butter

Microwave for one minute and whisk until smooth or melt and whisk in a double boiler, be careful not to let the chocolate get too hot.

Time: 10 minutes. Makes: 1/2 cup

This sauce is fabulous on ice cream and Black/White Truffle Profiteroles.

BLACK/WHITE TRUFFLE PROFITEROLES

Cream puffs (see page 69)

Ice Creams

> **Black Truffle Chocolate Ice Cream (see above)**
>
> **Vanilla Black Truffle Ice Cream (see page 66)**
>
> **White Truffle Espresso Ice Cream (see page 66)**

Black Truffle Chocolate Sauce (above)

Make the cream puffs bite size.

Use your favorite ice cream to fill the cream puffs.

Plate two or three filled cream puffs and top with warm Black Truffle Chocolate Sauce (see above).

CREAM PUFFS

1/2 cup butter

1 cup water

1/4 teaspoon salt

1 1/2 cups flour

5 eggs

My mother taught me to make Cream Puffs when I was six years old and they have been a favorite ever since.

Preheat oven to 350° In a saucepan bring butter, water, and salt to a boil. Add the flour and cook for two minutes stirring constantly. Remove from heat. Cool for 10 minutes. Add the eggs one at a time, beating well with a wooden spoon after each egg is added.

For larger cream puffs, drop by mounded tablespoon onto a greased cookie sheet 2 inches apart. For bite size cream puffs use a teaspoon.

Bake large puffs for 25 minutes and smaller ones for 20 minutes, until they are puffed and dry. Cool.

Slice open and fill with Black Truffle Chicken Salad for luncheon or heavy hors d'oeuvres. (see page 44)

Use for Black Truffle Profiteroles (see page 68)

Time: 45 minutes. Serves: 12 large or 24 small cream puffs

BLACK TRUFFLE CHOCOLATE HAZELNUT SPREAD

2 cups black truffle infused hazelnuts

1/4 cup baker's sugar

1 pound dark chocolate

1/2 cup black truffle infused butter

1 cup black truffle infused heavy cream

3/4 teaspoon salt

Melt chopped chocolate and sugar in a double boiler. Add truffle infused butter, stir to combine and slowly add the truffle infused cream and salt.

In a food processor, grind infused hazelnuts into a paste, add nut paste to the chocolate mixture, blend.

Put the spread in jars, it will thicken as it cools. Store in the refrigerator for up to a month. When ready to use let it stand at room temperature to soften.

Time: 30 minutes. Yield: 4-8 ounce jars

Try this with brioche, croissant, bread, scones, muffins or graham crackers.

BLACK TRUFFLE CHOCOLATE FONDUE

**12 ounces of chocolate
 (milk or dark, your choice)**

**8 ounces of black truffle
 infused heavy whipping cream**

Chop the chocolate. Heat the cream in a double boiler over medium heat until tiny bubbles show. Add the chocolate and stir until it is all incorporated.

Transfer to a fondue pot with a low flame or on low setting if electric.

Dippers can be your choice. I like fruits; strawberries, orange sections, bits of pineapple, mango, or bananas. Marshmallows and pieces of pound cake are also big hits.

Time: 10 minutes to prepare dippers
10 minutes to cook

Serves: 4

BLACK TRUFFLE HOT CHOCOLATE

www.foodandwine.com/slideshows/best-hot-chocolate lists Fran's Hot Chocolate one of the best in the U.S. Fran Bigelow of Seattle has been making chocolates for more than thirty years.

Absolutely the best hot chocolate is to use black truffle infused milk to make Fran's Hot Chocolate.

You could also make hot chocolate your favorite way, use cocoa powder and sugar or a commercial mix, but use black truffle infused milk.

For the ultimate, top with black truffle infused whipped cream!

BLACK TRUFFLE CHOCOLATE CAKE

2 cups all purpose flour

1 teaspoon salt

1 teaspoon baking powder

2 teaspoons baking soda

3/4 cup unsweetened cocoa
  powder

2 cups sugar

1 cup coffee

1 cup black truffle infused
  extra light olive oil

1 cup black truffle infused
  buttermilk

2 black truffle infused eggs

1 teaspoon vanilla

Preheat oven to 325°

In large mixing bowl whisk dry ingredients together. Add coffee, oil, and milk, mix well. Stir in eggs and vanilla and continue to mix for two more minutes. Meanwhile grease and flour 2 9-inch round cake pans. Pour batter into the prepared pans and bake for 30 minutes.

CHOCOLATE BLACK TRUFFLE ICING

4 cups confectioners sugar

1/4 cup unsweetened cocoa
  powder

1 cup black truffle infused
  butter, softened

3 tablespoons black truffle
  infused heavy whipping cream

1/2 teaspoon vanilla

In mixer, cream the truffle infused butter. Whisk together the sugar and cocoa powder and slowly add to the butter until smoothly combined. Mix in the whipping cream and vanilla.

Frost cooled cake.

Time: 2 hours including time to cool cake.

Serves 10

Resources

Bloomfield, A. and Goode, J. (2015) A Girl and her Greens: Hearty meals from the garden. United States: Ecco Press.

Kelly Slocum - Truffle Dogs (2015) Ty The Dog Guy, 17 February.

Carreiro, S. (2010) The Dog who Ate the Truffle: A memoir of stories and recipes from Umbria. United States: St. Martin's Press.

Cook, L. (2011) Fat of the Land: Adventures of a 21st century Forager. United States: Mountaineers Books.

Cook, L. (2013) The Mushroom Hunters: On the trail of an underground America. United States: Random House Publishing Group.

Czarnecki, J. (1995) A Cook's Book of Mushrooms: With 100 recipes for common and uncommon varieties. United States: Artisan Division of Workman Publishing.

Deur, D. (2014) Pacific Northwest Foraging: 120 wild and flavorful Edibles from Alaska blueberries to wild hazelnuts. United States: Timber Press (OR).

Editore, S.F. (2015) Discovering the Truffle: In history, in its habitat, in the kitchen. Italy: Slow Food Editore.

Hahn, J. (2010) Pacific Feast: A cook's guide to west coast foraging and cuisine. United States: Mountaineers Books, The.

Hall, I.R., Brown, G.T., Zambonelli, A. and Zambonelli, ra (2008) Taming the truffle: The history, lore, and science of the ultimate mushroom. Portland, Or.: Workman Publishing Company.

Lopez-Alt, K.J. (2015) The Food Lab: Better home cooking through science. United States: WW Norton & Co.

Luard, E. (2006) Truffles. United Kingdom:
Frances Lincoln Publishers.

lwdgifx, V.R.C. (2014) Overnight:
How to Teach Your Dog to Hunt Truffle.

Lyon, E. and Esthay, T. (2012) Truffle Hunting Dogs in Oregon.
Metcalfe, F. (2011) Truffle Hunting Practice.

Nowak, Z. (2015) Truffle: A Global History. United Kingdom:
Reaktion Books.

Safina, R., Sutton, J.C. and Safina, R. (2002) Truffles: Ultimate Luxury,
Everyday Pleasure. United States: John Wiley & Sons.

Schneider, K.R., Silverberg, R., Chang, A. and Schneider, R.G.M. (2015)
FSHN0406/FS104: Preventing Foodborne Illness: Clostridium
botulinum. Available at: http://edis.ifas.ufl.edu/fs104 (Accessed:
11 June 2016).

Trappe, M., Trapp, J., Evans, F. and Trappe, J.M. (2007) Field guide
to North American Truffles: Hunting, identifying, and enjoying the
world's most prized fungi. United States: Ten Speed Press.

Wells, P. (2011) Simply Truffles: Recipes and Stories that Capture the
Essence of the Black Diamond. United States: HarperCollins Publishers.

Wolf, B. (2014) Oregon truffle industry is beginning to bear fruit.
Available at: http://www.americanfoodroots.com/.../oregon_truffles_
start_getting.html (Accessed: 12 June 2016).

(No Date) Available at: http://YouTube Truffle Dog Training
www.NWTruffleDogs.com (Accessed: 15 June 2016).

Index

Made in the USA
Monee, IL
18 December 2020